INFOGRAPHIC GUIDE TO

Creating Stories

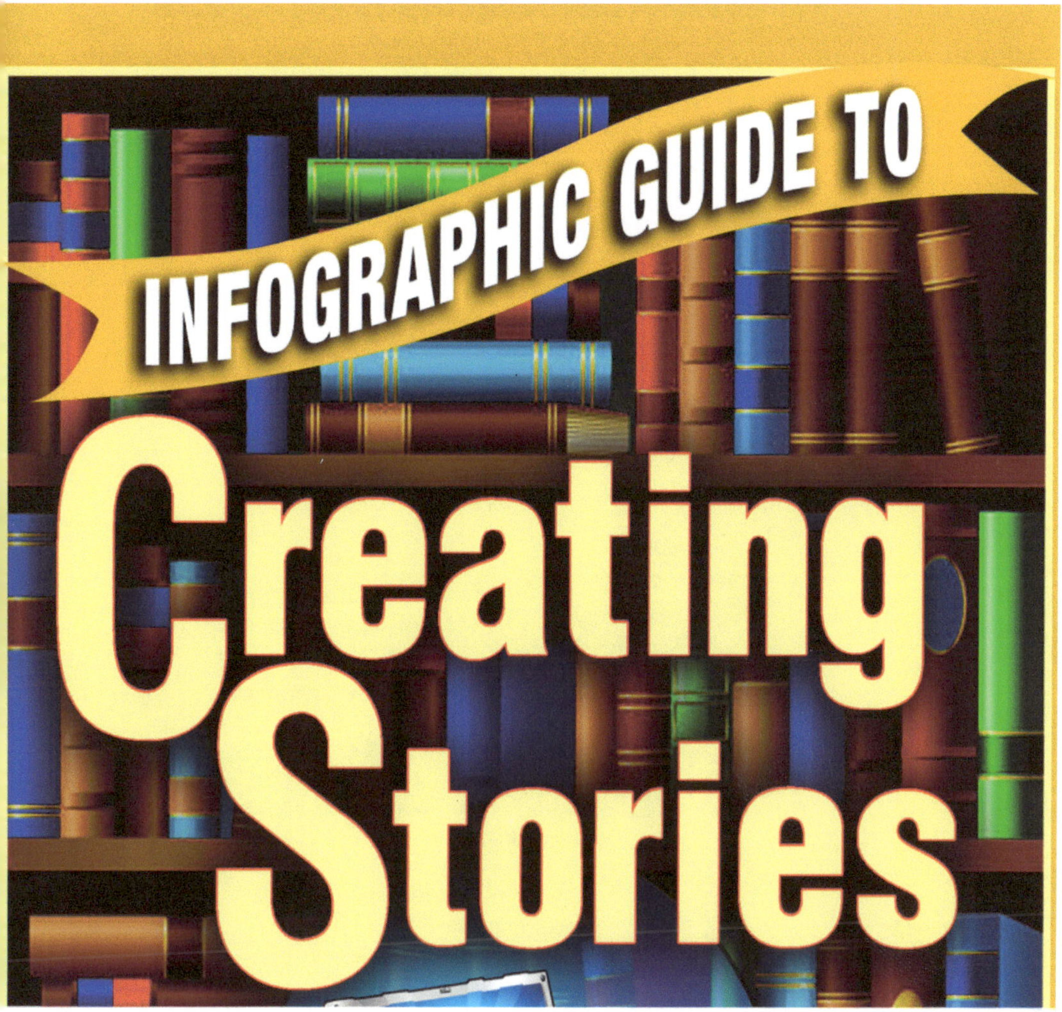

The Infographic Guide to Creating Stories

What others said about *Creating Stories*

Author Joylene Butler

This book is a true treasure and needs to be in the library of every writer worldwide.

Rene's Blog

Creating Stories is an excellent discourse on the essential elements of story crafting.

Author Mark Henderson

Hank doesn't purport to tell reader how to produce creative ideas, but offers guidance on how to turn those ideas into readable fiction.

Author Mark Cain

Creating Stories is highly recommended as a how-to guide for the novice writer

Emily-Jane Hills Orford for Readers' Favorite

For the wannabe writer who doesn't know where to start, this is the book for you.

ISBN: 9798985309737
Published in the United States of America.
Published by Strange Worlds Publishing

acknowledgments

The pages in this book were designed on the Canva
website: www.canva.com
The cover artist is Gary Tenuta: gvtgrafix@aol.com

Table of Contents

Foreword

This infographic book is designed to explain how one goes about creating a story -- a work of fiction -- from scratch. To put this in different words, suppose you suddenly get a strange idea and you think it'd make a great story. Well, why don't you write this great story? Why wait for someone else to write it? "But I don't how to write a story," you protest. This book will show you how to take that idea and turn it into an original story written by you.

Creating a Story

Let's take a look at how this story creation process will unfold. First, we'll go over a few basic ideas before we start with the story setting. Next you'll learn how to develop the characters in the story. After that, you'll see what is involved in putting together the story's plot. Then you'll gain an understanding about the importance of writing scenes. Finally, you'll learn some story-telling techniques followed by an understanding of how to fit all this stuff together.

Creativity

Creating your own story requires a lot of ideas. You'll need to be creative in other words. To do this, you have to remove all the mental blocks that build up over time. Think crazy thoughts. The crazier the better. When writing a story, crazy is good. Weird is even better. Boring is bad!

Chapter 1:
Getting Started

A few preliminary issues to discuss before we get started.

- *What is a story?*
- *Imagery*
- *Initial story idea*

A few words to kick off your amazng project.

Creativity

Writing a story requires a lot of ideas. You need ideas on the characters, plot events, setting and other stuff.

 ## Story idea

One of the first ideas you need is the initial story idea: something that triggers an urge to write a story.

Organization

You need a way to organize all your ideas. This book will do just that.

 ## Have fun!

Creating a story *can* be hard. The most important thing to remember is to have fun doing it!

WHAT IS A STORY?

A STORY IS ABOUT CHARACTERS WITH A PROBLEM IN A SETTING

CHARACTERS

Stories are always about characters, not events. If the story is about events it's history, not a story

PROBLEM

Solving the problem is the characters' job. It's what they do during the story

SETTING

The setting is where the story takes place and when it happens

SOUNDS SIMPLE, RIGHT?

Well, it isn't all that simple. But you can do it with the help of this book

You need imagery!

This is something you may not be aware of! But it's an essential part of creating a story

TV and movies

provide all the images the viewers need to understand what is going on.

Books

require the writer to provide descriptions. This requires image words and phrases.

Your story

must give the readers descriptions so they can build mental images about what is going on in the story.

Descriptions

are also required to understand the actions in the story.

The descriptions are required for the reader to "see" the settings and the actions.

HOW DO YOU CREATE A STORY?

#1 Stories are the result of three processes:

#2 ideas, story design and story-telling techniques.

#3 You need ideas on characters, plot events, scenes and much more.

#4 Story design is where you use your ideas to develop characters, plots, scenes and other stuff.

#5 Story-telling is where you tell the story in a way that holds the reader's interest.

INITIAL STORY IDEA

Where does the initial store idea come from? It can come from anywhere. My stories always start with a character but there are other ways a story can begin. Let's take a look at some.

A CHARACTER

You get an idea about an unusual character: an angry elf; a troll with a masters degree; a pet with superpowers. The next thing you know you think it'd be fun to write a story with that character.

A PLOT PROBLEM

This time you get an idea about big problem: such as how to eliminate world hunger. Or an evil superhero wants to conquer the world.

A SETTING

You see a picture of an old castle and you think "Wow, what a cool place. It'd be a great place to write a story about."

OTHER IDEAS

There are more ways to get an initial story idea besides the three I mentioned. Can you think of any?

ALL IDEAS ARE EQUAL

One way of starting a story is not better than another way. They are all equally great ways to begin

Chapter 2:
Story setting

Story setting is an important element in all stories.

Background

Setting is an essential part of the story design. Develop this early because the setting affects other elements in the story.

There are two types of setting in a story: the story setting and the scene setting. The scene setting is a subset of the story setting.

Where?

This is a basic detail. It affects many different aspects the story. How the characters dress, for instance. They'll need much different clothing if the story takes place in Antartica or in Florida.

When?

Another basic detail. This one can limit what the characters can do and what you can write about them. If the story takes place in ancient Rome, the characters can't know jujitsu or use a pistol.

Details

The details of the location are important to the readers. They make the story more interesting to them.
Write a few paragraphs of description on the setting so you don't confuse the details when you write the story.

Scenes

If the story setting is your town, then scenes can be in a park, a schoolyard, a mall, your friend's home, a church etc.

Story setting and scenes

Let's suppose your story setting is the Sahara desert. Then your scenes can be set in various places as shown in the sketch.

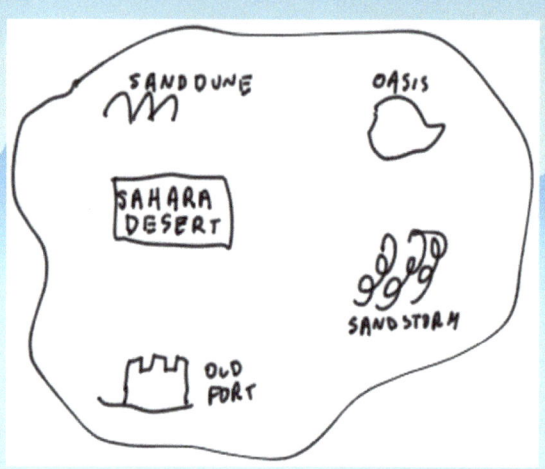

Make a sketch

If your scene setting will be used a few times, make a sketch so you don't move stuff around

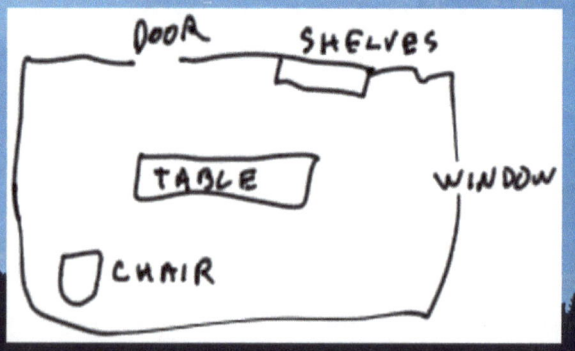

Chapter 3:
Character building

Fiction stories are about characters. Period.

- *Three buckets*
- *Physical bucket*
- *Mental bucket*
- *Biographical bucket*
- *Personality types*
- *Villains*
- *Personal philosophies*
- *Character arc*
- *Motivation*
- *Dominant reader emotion*
- *Character sheet*
- *Cast of characters*

Characters are the heart of your story.
To create a complete character, you have to fill
up three buckets with stuff.
A character doesn't have to be human.
It can be an elf, an alien, a rock. But it has to be able to
speak, think and experience emotions like a human.

PHYSICAL

This bucket is fairly easy to fill up. It tells the reader what the character looks like.

MENTAL

This bucket is a lot harder to fill up. Its about how the character thinks and reacts. This bucket is much more important than the physical bucket.

BIOGRAPHICAL

The more important a character is to the story, the more biographical material you need to come up with.

Why three buckets?

Because

These three buckets define your character. Real people (like you and your family and friends) have all three buckets. When people are very young the buckets are mostly empty. Over time the buckets become filled and will increase in size to reflect the experiences that folks accumulate as they go through life.

Limitations

As you decide on what goes into each bucket, you establish limits on your character and yourself as a writer.

If you select an optimist as a philosophy, your character can't act as a pessimist. In other words, she can't be constantly bad-mouthing other characters' opinions and ideas. If the character's personality is an adventurer, he can't be one who stays at home watching TV.

If the biography says the character didn't finish high school, she can't act and talk like she has a master's degree in engineering. If the bio says the character has a fear of dark places, he can't be excited about exploring a cave.

The physical attributes will also add limitations. If your character is skinny and weak, don't have him picking up large boulders or heavy objects to throw at the bad guy.

The Physical Bucket

The physical appearance bucket is straightforward and there is nothing tricky about it.

Appearance

provide information on the color of the character's skin, hair and eyes. Height, weight and build are also necessary

Clothing

This has to be realistic. You can't have a character wearing a ski jacket at the beach in the middle of summer, unless there is a reason for this bizarre development.

Tics

are habits that set the character apart from other characters in the story. An example is a woman who curls a hank of hair whenever she is thinking.

Speech

Does your character talk with a lisp? Does she stutter? Does she pepper her speech with foreign words? These bits of development can be used to make a character different from others.

Scars

A facial scar is a defining trait. So is a tattoo. Birthmarks or skin discoloration also fall into this category.

The Mental Bucket

Personality type

There are two sets of personalities you can use. One is for most characters and there is a special set for villains.

Personal Philosophy

Everybody has a personal philosophy. Whether you want one or not, you have it. And your characters need one.

Dreams &Memories

What do your characters dream about achieving? What do they aspire to become? How do their memories affect them?

Here's the thing

Much of this material will never make it directly into the story. But it allows you to get the characters to act, react and think like real people (even if they're not human).

Ready?

You'll figure this stuff out on the next few pages.

Character Biography

A biography for the character serves a dual purpose. Besides providing background information, it allows the author to understand the character and that understanding is vital when dealing with the character in stressful situations.

Introduction

Write a paragraph or two about each topic listed. The more you add , the better you'll understand the character

Family

Describe the character's family life. Parents, siblings? Married? Kids? Where does she live?

Career

Jobs, military experience? Does he like what he does? Why or why not?

Education

Schools, degrees, favorite subject? Depending upon the age of the character, the amount of schooling will vary

Experiences

Combat? Injuries? Sports? Hobbies? Arrested? Divorced?

Fears

What does the character fear? Dark places? Open water? Aliens? Something else?

PERSONALITY TYPES

There are four general categories here, each with four sub-types

Analysts

Intuitive and thinking personality types known for their rationality, impartiality and intellectual excellence.

Diplomats

intuitive and feeling personality types known for their empathy, diplomatic skills and passionate idealism.

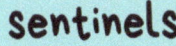

sentinels

Observant and judging personality types known for their practicality and focus on order, stability and security.

Explorers

Observant and prospecting personality types known for their spontaneity, ingenuity and flexibility.

Research

Each of these four personality types have four sub-types. To see those and learn more about each type, go to: https://www.16personalities.com/personality-types

VILLAINS

Your antagonist can be regular person and have a personality type like on the previous page. However, if you want the antagonist to be a really bad guy, use one of these villain types instead.

Evil Overlord
At the top of a power pyramid and wants still more power.

Obsessed Scientist
Intelligent, analytical, creative and determined.

The Sadist
Motivation is pleasure at victims' pain or fear.

The Bully
Picks on vulnerable victims. Motivated by the short term power boost his ego gets.

The Social Reject
Outside society. Maybe an outlaw, a nerd or misfit.

The Smothering Mother
Dominates her family or community or club.

From Rayne Hall's: Writing About Villains.

PERSONAL PHILOSOPHY

Everyone has one of these.
You'll have to give each important character a personal philosophy. Once you assign a personality and a philosophy, you create a set of limitations that you'll have to observe.

INDIVIDUALISM

Philosophical theory emphasizing personal freedom and autonomy.

HEDONISM

A doctrine of pleasure as the highest or only good.

MATERIALISM

Reality consists solely of matter without separate reality of mind or spirit.

OPTIMISM

Doctrine holding that reality is fundamentally good and the world is governed by benign forces.

PESSIMISM

Reality is fundamentally evil and the world is governed by malevolent forces.

PRAGMATISM

Emphasizes consequences and practical results of one's conduct rather than principles and categories of reality.

SCEPTICISM:

Theory that man can never attain certain knowledge and that all knowledge should be questioned.

Adding a philosophy to your characters is an important step in making them "real" to the reader. It also means you are getting to know your characters better. There are many more philosophies than these, but these are the most common.

Character Arc

If there is no character arc then everything after the story ends is the same as before the story began. Nothing happened, in other words. The only thing that changed is that the characters got older. A story without a character arc is an incomplete and unsatisfactory story.

There are two types of character arcs. One concerns itself with what great lesson the main character(s) learn over the course of the story. The second is what changes in the life of the character(s) as a result of the events in the story.

The character arc can be physical or mental or both, but a mental character arc is more interesting than a physical one. In a mental character arc, the character learned an important lesson. In a physical one, the character's situation changed for better or worse.

To get a deeper understanding for character arcs, we can look at a few examples.
- A character starts out as a bigot but during the course of the story learns to be less bigoted and becomes more open-minded.
- A proud or pompous (or both) character gets humbled as the story unfolds.
- A lazy character gets motivated.
- A character evolves from an uninterested bystander or a follower into the leader of a movement.

Here are examples of a great character arc from the movies.
- In Star Wars, Luke Skywalker evolves from a rustic farm boy into a Jedi knight (and it only took three movies for that to happen).
- In Lord of the Rings, both the books and the movies, Frodo evolves. As a result of his journey, he changes from an inexperienced youth to a strong-minded, decisive man (or hobbit, to be more precise).

The character arc applies to the antagonist as well as the protagonist. That assumes the bad guy is still alive after the story ends. If the antagonist is dead, well, maybe he did learn something, but it was a bit too late to be useful.

Motivation-1

Character motivation is essential

1

Think about your protagonist. He has to solve a plot problem. That's the character's job. Your character has to get up off the couch, go out into the cruel world and possibly risk his life in order to solve the problem.
Why should he go through all this effort?

2

That's the question you, the author, have to answer. What's the character's motivation? Why does he feel he has to solve the problem? Why doesn't he say, "Let someone else do it." Or, "I'm too busy." Or, "Maybe I'll do it later."

3

You can't have a half-hearted effort to track down a serial killer. Nor can you have an all-out effort by the entire cast to find a Mother's Day card. If the characters are risking their lives, the motivation has to reflect the seriousness of the situation.

4

Simply put, motivation is what drives the protagonist to solve the plot problem and it's what drives the antagonist to struggle to prevent the good guy from succeeding. Both the protagonist and the antagonist have to be motivated and these two motivations have to be commensurate in strength.

Motivation-2

Character motivation is essential

A complex character, the kind readers love, should have both outer and inner motivation. The outer motive is fairly easy to develop. It is usually based on solving the plot problem. Once this problem is resolved, the outer motive has been met.

The inner motive is more complicated. It can be almost anything and doesn't have to be related to the plot problem.

The best combination of motives is a pair of mutually exclusive ones; the protagonist can't achieve one without giving up the other.

This constraint sets up natural internal conflict in the character and can lead to unexpected plot twists that will keep the reader involved. Effectively, the author has constructed an engine of motivation and anti-motivation.

Dominant Reader Emotion (DRE)

This isn't part of the character's inner or outer aspects. It also isn't part of the character's biography. The Dominant Reader's Emotion (DRE) is the emotion you want (hope!) the reader will experience whenever the character is in a scene.

Whatever reader emotion you choose dictates the way you write about the character and limits what you can have the character do

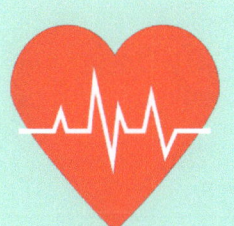

If you want a character to be *sympathetic to* a reader, you can't create a willful, powerful, egotistical character because it will be difficult for a reader to be sympathetic to such a character.

If you want the reader to *like* a character, you can't have him kicking puppies or pushing little old ladies in front of buses. You can have a character do these things if the reader emotion you're striving for is *anger* or *disgust*.

Dominant Reader Emotions

Affection	The reader develops a fondness or liking for the character.
Delight	The reader takes pleasure in the character and her actions.
Anger	The reader feels displeasure with the character.
Disgust	The reader is revolted by the character.
Empathy	The reader relates to the character and thinks the character is just like the reader.
Irritation	The reader is annoyed by the character.
Sadness	The reader feels sorry or unhappy for the character
Pity	The reader feels sorry for the character.

CHARACTER SHEET

There is a lot of stuff involved in building character. You need a way to keep track of all of the material. Copy the items below into a word processor form and save it. Make a copy for each character in your story.

Character Name: ¶
Story Function: ¶
Physical Attributes ¶
Physical Traits: ¶
Biographical Material: ¶
Dress Habits: ¶
Dialog: ¶
Mental Attributes ¶
Philosophy ¶
Personality Type ¶
Dreams (Aspirations) ¶
Memories that influence the motivation ¶
Mirages that a character fools himself into believing ¶
Other Attributes ¶
Character Arc ¶
Motivation ¶
Dominant Reader Emotion

CAST OF CHARACTERS

Remembering everything about all the characters in the story is a bit of a chore. It helps to have a cheat sheet. You can use the one below. Copy the items into a spreadsheet or make a table in a word processor to use it. The sample character will help you to understand the listings.

	Story Title:		Cast of Characters © 2020 Hank	
Design Information	**Character 1**	**Character 2**	**Sample character**	**Character 3**
General				
Name			Angus MacDrakin	
Role			Antagonist	
Occupation			Gem miner	
Eductation			Can read, write and do numbers	
Physical Aspects				
Race			Dwarf	
Skin color			olive complexion	
Eye color			black	
Hair color & length			black, long	
Beard color & length			black, shaggy	
Height			3-10	
Weight			163	
Stature			stocky, barrel-shaped	
Distinguishing marks			Scar on forehead	
Clothing			green & back tartan kilt, leather vest, boot	
Speech			loud	
Dialog			Slight Scottish accent	
Mental Aspects				
Personality type	Analyst		Explorer	
Personality sub-type			Adventurer	
Traits			strong-willed, stubborn, excitable	
Dominant Reader Emotion			annoyance	
Character Arc				
Starting			rich. arrogant	
Ending			poor, humble	

Chapter 4: Plotting

The plot is what gives the characters a job.
It tells the characters what to do.

- *Constructing a plot*
- *Three failures*
- *Plot example*
- *Cheat sheet*
- *The climax*
- *Subplots*

Developing a plot requires a lot of creativity and thinking. You may not be able to complete it right away. The plot you build must be one that YOU believe in. If you don't, you'll never be able to convince the reader to believe in it. The plot has a four-part purpose

1. Drives the characters

The plot gives the characters a job and tells them how to go about doing the job. The plot moves the characters forward.

2. Provides conflict

The conflict doesn't have to be limited to the protagonist versus the antagonist. The conflict should be expanded to involve more characters. The more conflicts going on, the better.

The conflict builds tension among the characters. For instance, the hero and his friend are getting stressed out by their constant bickering over how to approach the plot problem.

3. Builds tension

4. Unleashes emotions

The more conflict there is and the more serious the situation becomes, the stronger the characters' emotions have to be. You can't have a protagonist fail a few times and have a lackluster emotional response.

Ready?

Let's go!

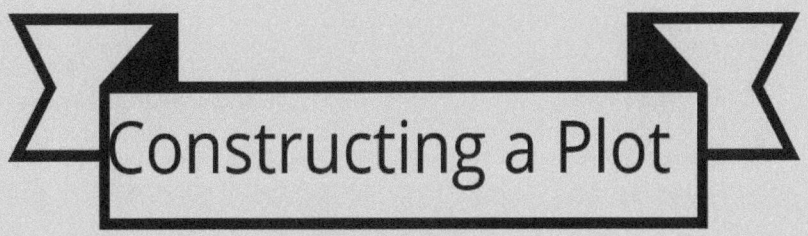

Constructing a Plot

Plot Definition

A plot is a series of important events that connect the story's beginning (inciting event) with the story's ending (climax) .

Plot Development Process

Developing a plot is a three-step process:
1. Get a plot problem
2. Find the story's ending
3. Create a series of logical events that connect steps 1 and 3

Step 2

Isn't intuitive, but it is necessary. You can't develop Step 3 until you know what Step 2 is. If you try to develop Step 3 without knowing what Step 2 is, you don't know where the story's ending is and consequently, you don't know what events you need.

Constructing a Plot

Step 2 is tough. Coming up with the story ending isn't easy and requires a bit of creativity. You may no be able to come with the ending right away. It may take some time before you are able to find the endin

Step 3 is really hard because of the plot cloud. You don't know what the plot cloud is?

Think of a vast cloud or chamber filled with an infinite number of possible plot events. That is the plot cloud. All you know are the two end points. You know nothing in between. Now you have to construct a path throght this cloud to connect the inciting evert with the climax.

Constructing a Plot

Since there are an infinite number of possible events in the plot cloud, there are also an infinite number of possible plot paths to connect the inciting events and the climax

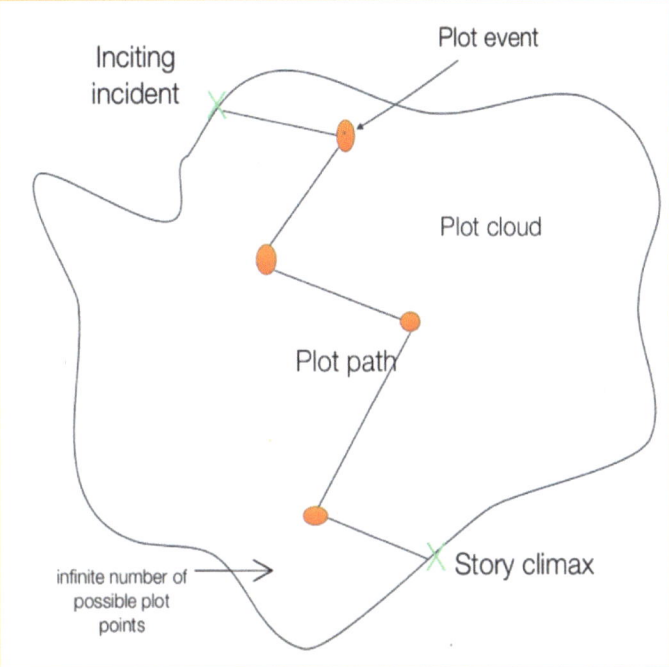

Your job is to come up with a plot path through the cloud. It must be logical and it must be one that you believe in. If you can't believe in it, you'll have to dump it and start over.

Constructing a Plot

The protagonist must try to solve
the plot problem three times
and must fail each time.

Why three times?

On the first page of this chapter,
it was stated that the purpose
of the plot is to drive the characters,
provide conflict, build tension and
unleash emotions.
All of these purposes are
accomplished through the failures.

THREE

FAILURES

1 THE HERO

makes a half-hearted attempt to solve the problem and fails. She is surprised and understands the problem isn't so easy to fix.

2 ONCE AGAIN,

she makes an attempt, This time she puts more effort into it. The failure alarms her and she realizes she is in trouble with the problem

3 FOR THIS

attempt, she puts everything she has into the effort. The failure throws her into despair.

Now the hero and the story are set up for the climax: the hero's do-or-die attempt.

At this point, the hero is as emotionally low as she can get.

The Climax

This has to be the best part of the story and your best writing. If the reader remembers anything about the story, it should be the climax.

Emotionally, the hero is as low as she can get.

Meanwhile, the bad guy's emotions have soared. They are as high as possible.

The hero is determined to fix the problem. The bad guy is determined to make the hero fail.

Someone has to win! There are no ties in a story. There has to be a winner and a loser.

After the climax, there is one more scene to explain what the winner achieved.

Noteworthy!

The two characters have to give everything they have in the climactic scene. They can't mail it in.

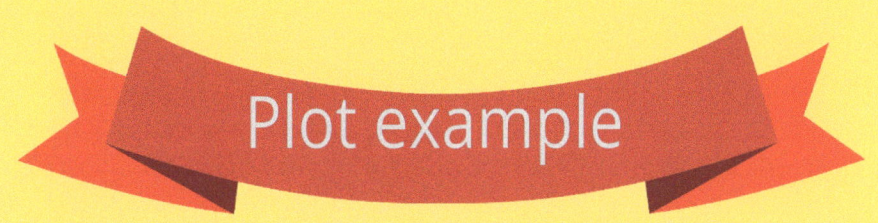

Plot example

Let's engage in an exercise to illustrate how a plot can come together.
Chris, the protagonist, has a treasure map and he's determined to find the treasure. Getting it is the plot problem.
Jack, the antagonist, knows about the treasure and the map and he's determined to get it before Chris does. This is the plot's beginning or the inciting incident.

After some thought, you decide on the ending: Chris will find and take the treasure. The graphical representation of the plot at this point looks like this.

Chris		
Jack		Treasure

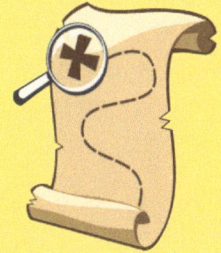

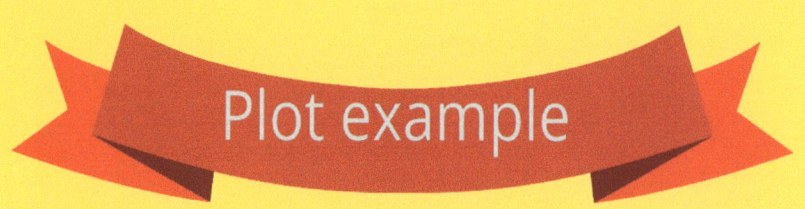

Plot example

The problem you now have is to figure out how to get the characters to the location of the treasure.
To complicate matters, you add another character, Ann, an FBI agent, who believes the treasure is loot from a bank robbery. Ann's story can be a subplot or part of the main storyline. Now the diagram looks like this.

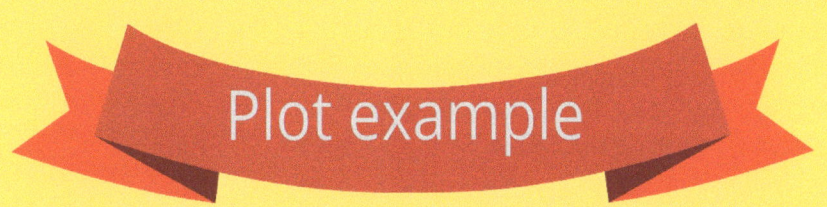

Plot example

After some thought, you decide Chris and Jack will move toward the treasure and bump into each other on the way. This will be the first event. Chris fails to get rid of Jack and Jack doesn't get rid of Chris.

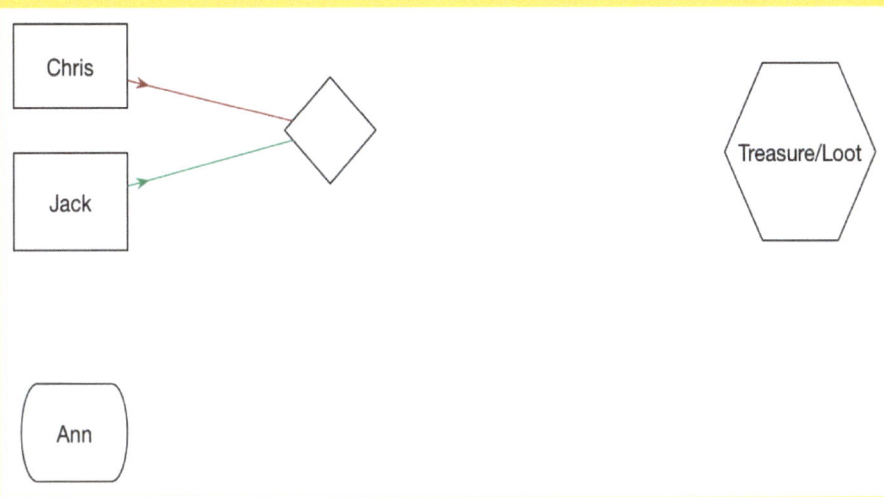

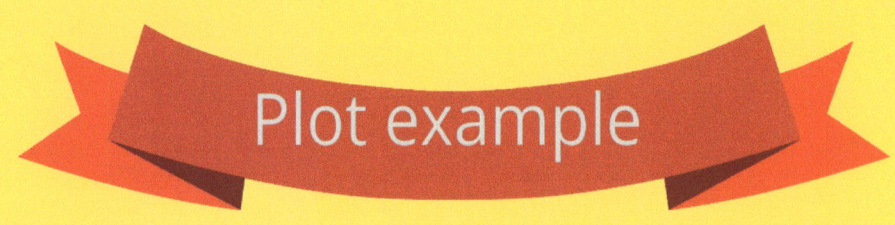

Next, you come up with another plot event: Jack and Ann will collide as they both move toward the treasure.

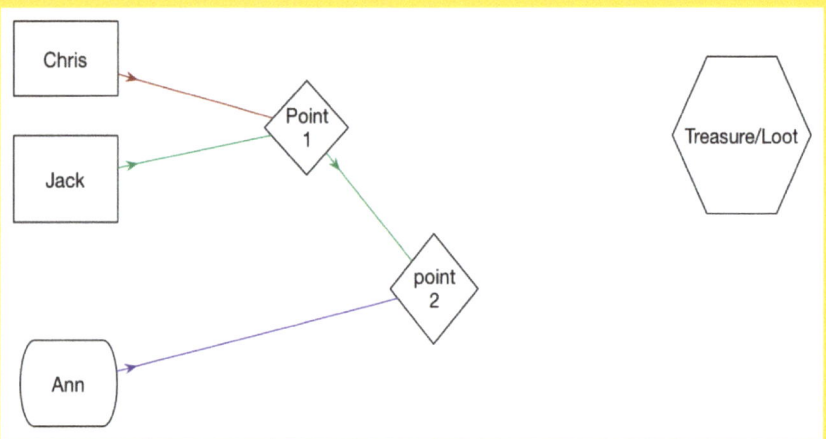

The events at Points 1 and 2 have to be action scenes. The characters have to do more than hide from each other or wave a hand in greeting. There has to be action: a fist fight, a gun battle, a car chase (or a horse chase if it's a Western). Something dramatic has to happen, something to show conflict, tension and emotions. This is your chance to show the reader your writing chops.

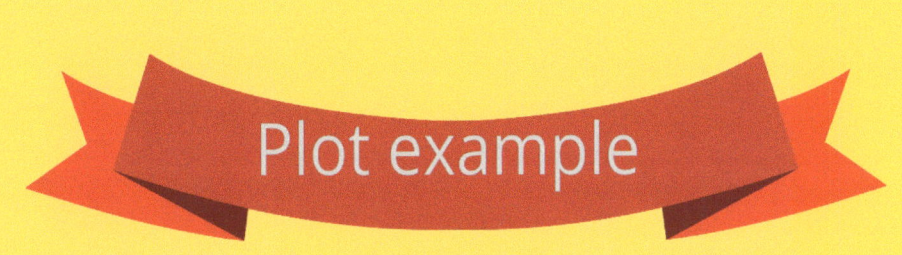

After the conflict at Points 1 and 2, the plot gets tricky. Your next job is to get Chris, Jack and Ann to the location of the treasure. But they all have to arrive at the same time. This requires a bit of planning to ensure that the timing of the characters' journey is in sync so one of them doesn't arrive too early or too late.   Once they all arrive, you've reached the climax of your story. It won't be much of a climax if Chris arrives, gets the treasure and leaves before Jack gets there, finds out the treasure is gone and leaves before Ann shows up. Sequential arrivals won't cut it. That could happen in real life, but this is fiction, not real life.

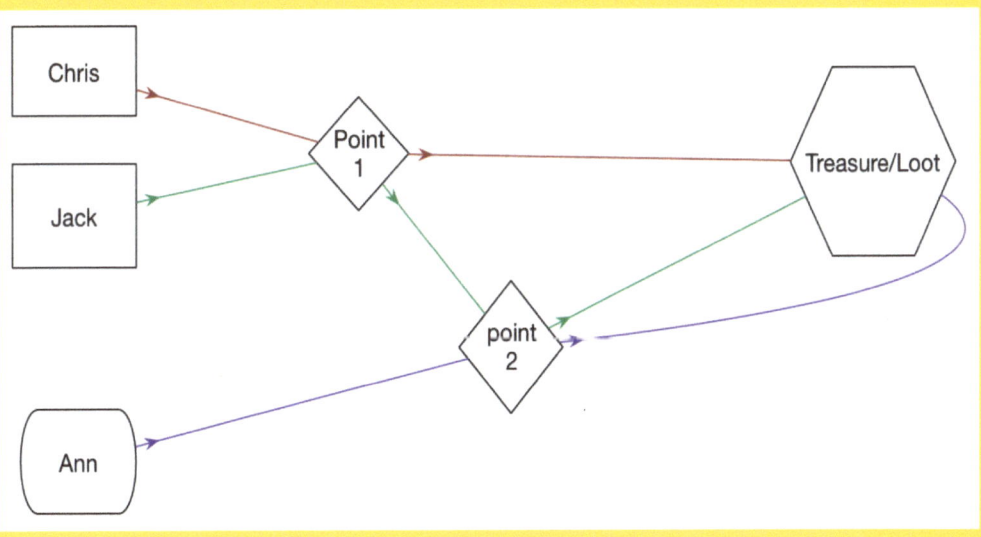

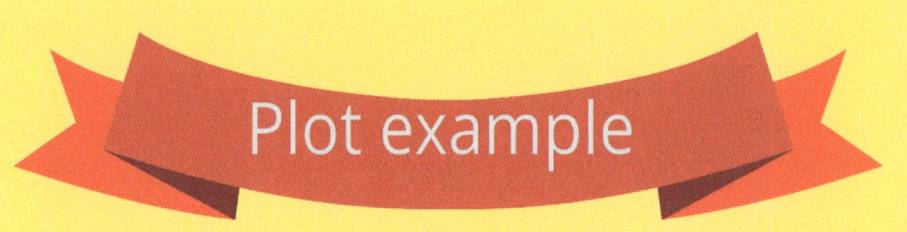

Once the characters get to the treasure/loot location you have the setup for a great amount of conflict. You can have Chris versus Jack; Chris versus Ann; Jack versus Ann; Ann versus both of the guys. You can have Chris and Ann team up against Jack. You can have Chris and Jack join forces against Ann or even Jack and Ann against Chris. However you arrange the conflicts and the ending, remember you also need tension and emotions.

This example is simplified. There is only one failure for Chris and Jack. The conflict at Points 1 and 2 is about eliminating the competition. The complete plot would have many more conflict points in it.

This plot example can be used in a number of variations. If the treasure is replaced by Chris' kidnapped daughter, you have a completely different story. If you write mystery stories, the treasure may be the point where all the clues come together to resolve the mystery.

Plotting
CHEAT SHEET

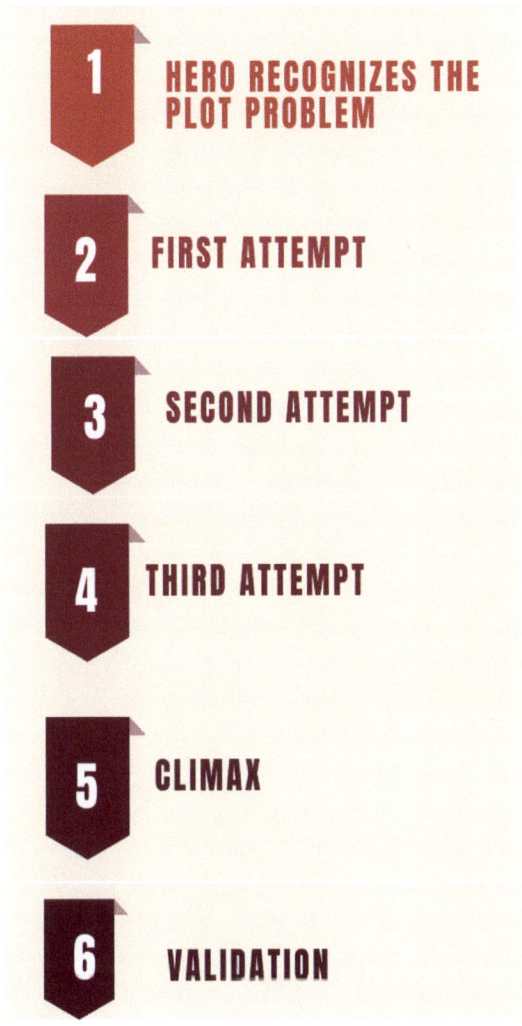

1. **HERO RECOGNIZES THE PLOT PROBLEM**

2. **FIRST ATTEMPT**

3. **SECOND ATTEMPT**

4. **THIRD ATTEMPT**

5. **CLIMAX**

6. **VALIDATION**

In a short story, these steps could be the scenes in the story. In a longer work, each step could be several chapters.

Subplots

Subplots have a number of uses. Here is a list of the main ones.

01

Distract the reader
While the reader is engrossed in the subplot, the sneaky main characters are off doing something that will surprise the reader when she finds out what they did.

02

Give the reader a break
If the plot is especially intense, the readers will appreciate a break. The subplot gives them a chance to catch their breath and cool off a bit.

03

Stretch out the tension
The subplots make the main plot seem longer, stretching out the tension.

04

Build anticipation
This stretching out with subplots will build the anticipation of the reader to reach the climax.

05

Explore and develop other characters
The subplots can be used to explore less important characters and give the readers insights into these characters.

06

Provide foreshadowing
A subplot can be used to show a development that seemingly is independent of the main plot but is actually a crucial element in the climactic scene.

Chapter 5: Scene design

Stories consist of scenes.
- *Scene goal*
- *Scene arc*
- *Sensory information*
- *Scene setting*
- *Emotional arc*

Scenes are the building blocks of the story -- not sentences, not paragraphs, not chapters -- scenes. You create a story by writing one scene at a time.

But

Scenes have to be designed to fit the story. A scene must either characterize a character or move the reader closer to the climax.

Goal

Every scene **must** have a goal for the characters in that scene to try and achieve. Even if the scene is characterizing a character, there **must** be a goal

Arc

The point of view character in the scene **must** undergo an emotional change during the scene.

Setting

Every scene has a setting that is a subset of the story setting.

Senses

Sensory information should always be included in each scene.

Scene Goal

The purpose of a story is to take the reader on a journey. That journey is made up of scenes. To satisfy this requirement the scene must have a goal. The scene can't simply be a collection of paragraphs clumped together for the author's convenience.

In a short story, the scene goal is usually related to solving the plot problem. In a novel, the scene goal can be related to a number of objectives.

Typical examples of scene goals are to get vital information, to reach a specific location, to identify someone. These goals are waypoints in the movement of the story. Some scene goals may be accomplished within a single scene or the goal may require several scenes before it is reached or completed. For instance, to reach the specific location can take many scenes, each one moving the characters closer to the location.

When you characterize someone, you are describing his background, or part of his biography, or spending time inside his head as he ponders how to solve a problem. This last bit is known as internal monologue and is a powerful way to pass information on to the reader as the character thinks about his situation.

A goal, such as reaching a location, can be the objective of an entire part of the story involving a number of chapters. Many of the scenes will involve overcoming obstacles such as werewolves or a rain-swollen river or a holiday traffic jam. In a quest story, reaching the location can be the goal of the entire story.

Scene arc

Readers want to experience and share the characters' emotional journey. In order to create this emotional journey, each scene must have an emotional change in it. What this means is that the character's emotion at the end of the scene must be changed from the character's emotion at the start of the scene. Whether the change is positive or negative is irrelevant. A scene with a flat emotional arc is not a good scene

Emotional arcs:

Here are examples of emotional arcs that can occur within a scene. Use them as is or reverse them.

- content to annoyed
- annoyed to angry
- angry to enraged
- depressed to relieved
- happy to sad
- nervous to calm
- indifference to irritation
- denial to acceptance
- excitement to dread

Sensory Information

We're surrounded by stuff our senses pick up. The sight and colors in a rainbow or a camp fire. The look on the face of a delighted child. The smell of newly mown grass. The sound of traffic or the sound of birds or heavy metal bands. The touch of a child's hand or a smack in the face. The feel of a kiss or the thrill of a hug.

These are all part of being alive. They are part of our humanity. So, your job as a writer is to make sure the reader shares the sensory information that the characters experience in the scene.

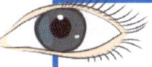

Sight is always shared with readers; it's how the character tells the reader what's going on in the scene. But that isn't enough.

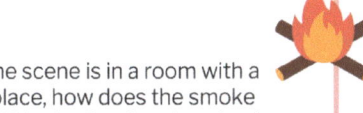

If the scene is in a room with a fireplace, how does the smoke smell? Is the fireplace burning logs from an apple tree?   Does the smoke hurt the character's throat?

If the scene is in a wooded area, Is there the sound of small animals scurrying around in the underbrush? Birdsong? Chattering of squirrels? How about the earthy smell of decomposing leaves?

If the scene is set in Manhattan the reader has to "hear" the rumble of traffic, the piercing scream of fire engine sirens, the staccato sounds of construction.

Without sensory information, the scene will seem sterile to the reader.

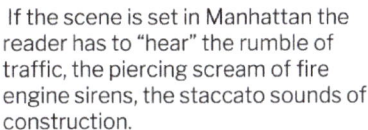

SCENE
SETTING

The scene setting is a subset of the story setting.

The important issue here is that you give the reader the words necessary to build an image of the scene setting.

If the setting is your town, then scenes can be in the school yard, at home, in the park. at the mall.

If the location is used more than once, you don't have to repeat the details unless something changed.

Besides the location, the setting details can include the weather and the season, the time of day (or night) and any other pertinent information.

Emotional Arc-1

If you've ever been on the edge of your seat when the climax of the movie approaches, you've experienced an emotional arc. If you ever stayed up late at night reading a story, you have also been hooked by the story's emotional arc. All stories require an emotional arc.

The character's emotional change in a scene must start with the ending emotion in the previous scene, and the ending emotion in the new scene becomes the beginning emotion in the succeeding scene. In other words, the emotional changes form a continuous arc that stretches from the story's opening scene to the climatic scene at the end. Stories with multiple main characters will have multiple emotional arcs, one for each main character.

In the example below, the starting emotion for Scene Y is the same as the ending emotion in Scene X. And Scene Z picks up where Scene Y left off. This example is for a single character. With multiple main characters and emotional arcs, this continuous arc would be interrupted by the scenes from the other emotional arcs. Thus, keeping track of each character's emotional arc is yet another chore for the author, but it is an important one.

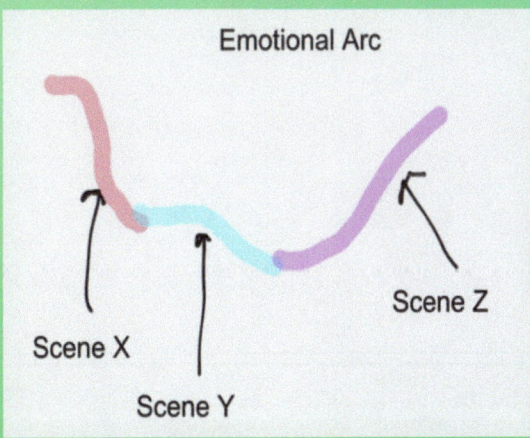

For a short story, developing this arc is relatively simple because of the small number of scenes involved. The situation is more complicated in a novel because of the many scenes involved and the multiple points of view and subplots.

Emotional Arc-2

Let's simplify this mind-boggling concept. The emotional arc I'll describe belongs to a single character, not the entire cast. However, each major character needs his own emotional arc. Yeah, that's right. Both the antagonist and the protagonist need an emotional arc. The sidekicks can and should have one also, especially if they star in their own subplots.
This arc is typical in a quest or adventure story. Other types of stories will have different emotional arcs.

A story's emotional arc is a product of the scene designs melded to the plot events. The purpose of the emotional arc is to grip the reader and keep her reading even though it's past her bedtime.
To explain this concept, I'll use a series of graphs to illustrate the emotional changes as the story progresses.

Emotional Arc-3

To begin, here is the basic structure of the graph. As you see, the vertical axis is used to record the character's emotional state, both positive and negative, while the horizontal axis shows time within the story.

Plot events and emotional arcs

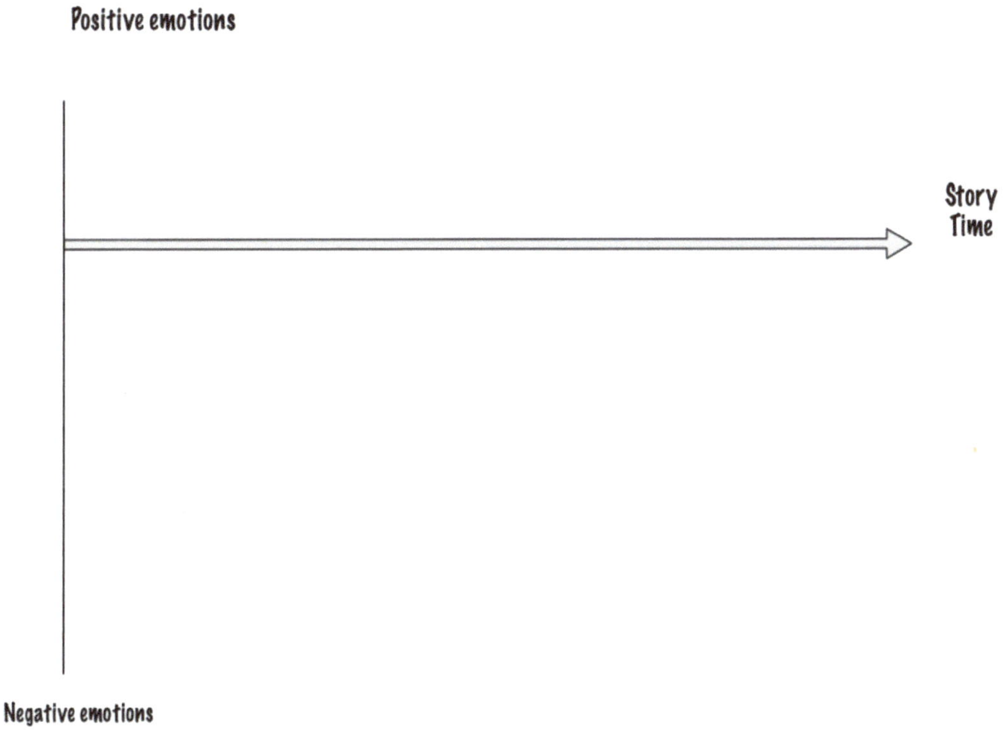

Positive emotions

Story
Time

Negative emotions

Emotional Arc-4

In this chart the red line depicts the emotional curve you'll find in stories created by new writers. Essentially, it's a flat line, an indication of little if any emotional changes in the story. For contrast, my emotional curve for the first draft is shown in green. It's much steeper than the red line, but it can still use some sharpening and improvement. That's what second and third drafts are for, improving the emotional curve (and fixing typos among other chores).

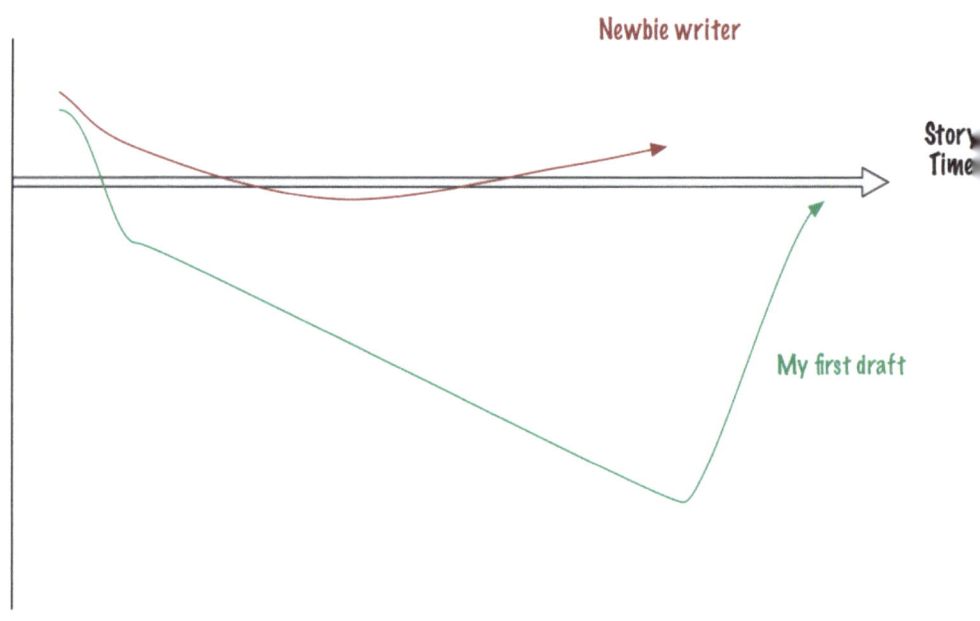

Plot events and emotional arcs

Positive emotions

Newbie writer

Story Time

My first draft

Negative emotions

Emotional Arc-5

With the basics out of the way, we can now construct an emotional curve as your story unfolds. I'll explain this one step at a time. In this chart, the story begins with the protagonist in a positive emotional state. Life is good, he's cool, everything is grand.

Then he recognizes the plot problem and his emotional state drops a bit lower. He's not quite as happy as he was. "Why me?" he moans. "I don't have time for this stuff." But then he thinks of a way to solve the problem and his emotional state improves. He puts his plan into action and it fails. "Uh-oh, this isn't as easy I thought it would be." This failure results in a drop in his emotional level.

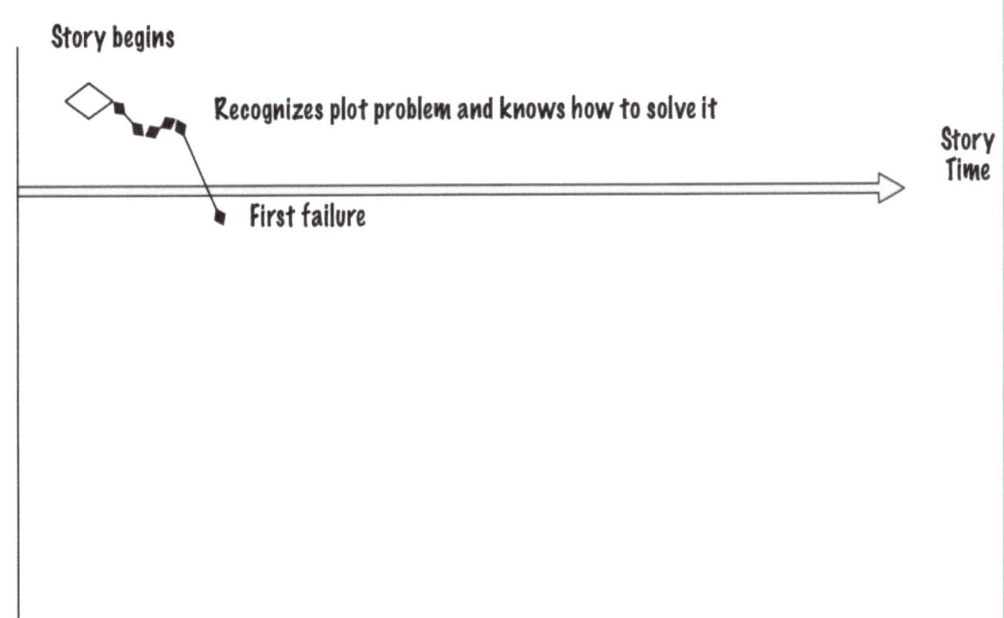

Plot events and emotional arcs

Story begins

Recognizes plot problem and knows how to solve it

Story Time

First failure

Negative emotions

Emotional Arc-6

The hero ponders the situation and comes up with another plan.
. His second attempt also fails and now he's getting alarmed. His emotiona
state plunges deeper into negative territory.
These attempts can be a single scene or they can involve a number of scene
but each scene has to result in a change in the emotional state.

Plot events and emotional arcs

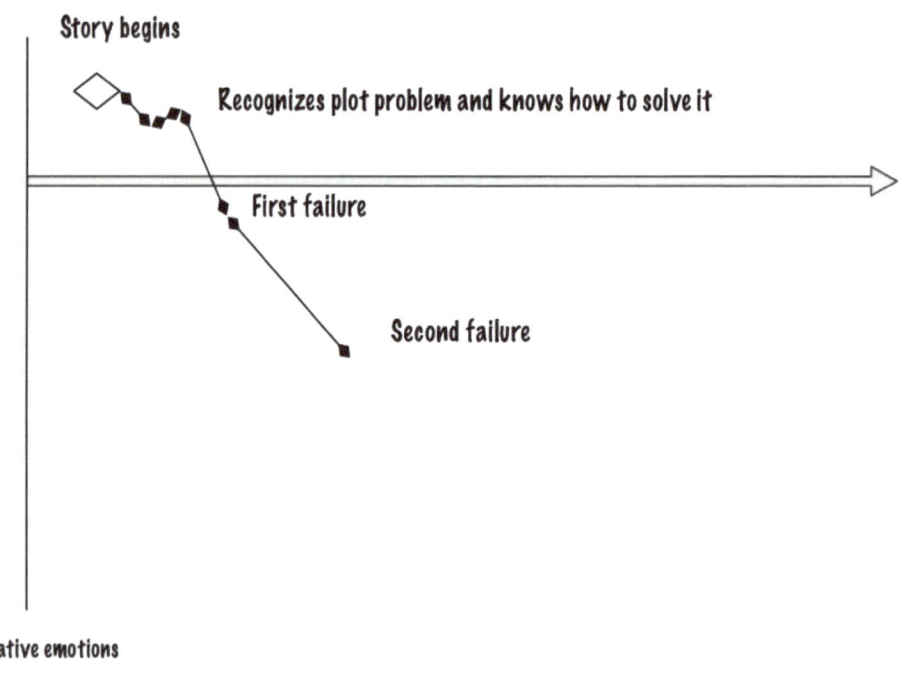

Emotional Arc-7

Struggling on, the hero develops still another plan and executes it. Again he fails and his emotional state has now sunk into depression. After wallowing around for a while, he sucks it up and decides he'll solve the problem or die trying. At this point, your story has reached the beginning of the climax.

Plot events and emotional arcs

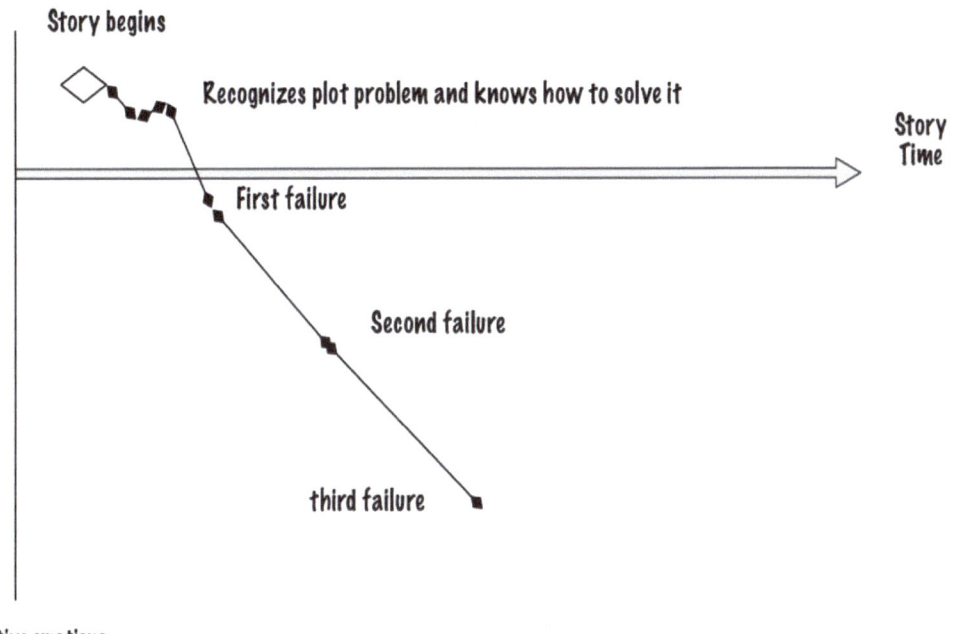

Emotional Arc-8

I'm sure you've watched a movie that had you on the edge of your seat toward the end. You're biting your nails wondering how the hero can get out of the mess he's in. In this case, the director has set you up for the movie's big climactic scene. That's what you, the author, must do with your story and the readers. You have to get the readers anxious to find out how the hero will survive/solve/whatever the next scene. As the hero struggles through the climactic scene, his emotional state soars (or not, if he doesn't succeed, which is always an option).

Plot events and emotional arcs

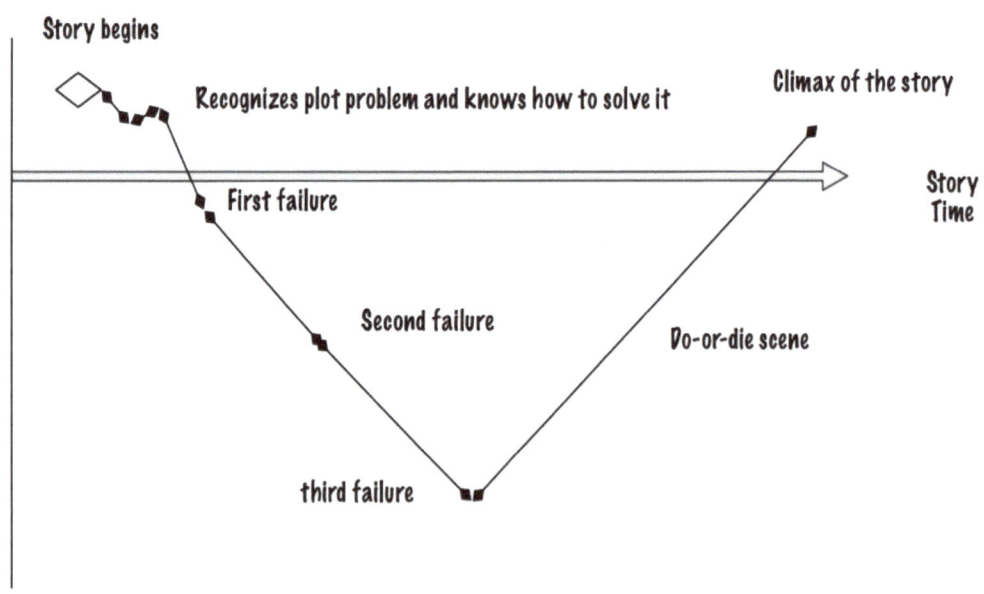

Emotional Arc-9

Don't forget, the climactic scene must be followed by the validation scene.

The charts presented here depict the hero's emotional journey. The bad guy also has an emotional journey and it's the exact opposite of the good guy's journey. Every time the protagonist fails, the antagonist wins and his emotional state shoots up while the protagonist's falls.

This overall process of constructing an emotional arc is how a compelling story is put together. Whether you draw a chart, use an outline or a mind-map, you have to track these emotional changes in order to properly develop the story's emotional arc. It won't do to have the protag's emotional arc bounce around and go positive before the story's ending. In this case, the arc is out of whack. The protag's emotions can improve and tick upward (slightly) but this has to be a temporary situation and his downward spiral must continue soon afterward.

For a short story, each of the failures can be a scene. In a longer work, each failure can be one or more chapters long or even an entire act.

Chapter 6:
Story-telling

No matter how creative your ideas are and no matter how great your story design is, if the story doesn't hold the reader's interest, the story is a failure. This chapter will discuss ways to grab the reader and hold her attention.

- *Point of view*
- *Stimulus and reaction*
- *Show-don't-tell*
- *Foreshadowing*
- *Metaphor and similes*

POINT OF VIEW

Point of view (POV) and the Emotional Arc are the most technical aspects of creating a story.

1

It's your baby

You're the author. You created the story, the characters, the plot, the scenes. Now you have to make a choice about how the story is told to the reader.

2

Omniscient POV

Previously, stories were told in the omniscient point of view. In other words, the author told the story.   As a way of telling an entire story this mode is obsolete. Nowadays, it's common to use omniscient POV in a limited way such as describing the scene setting.

3

Other POVs

Today, the story is usually told from a character's POV. The most common point of view choices are third person limited and first person.

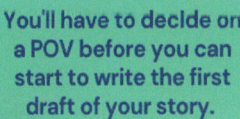

You'll have to decide on a POV before you can start to write the first draft of your story.

Once you decide on a POV to use, you'll have to stick with it throughout the entire story.

Omniscient POV Example

The old forest was gloomy and humid. Not even a hint of a breeze stirred the leaves. Occasionally a small shaft of sunlight broke through and illuminated a small patch of ground. Vines hung from the lower limbs of the huge oak trees and thick spider webs filled in the spaces between vines and limbs.

In this case the narrator is the author telling the reader what the forest looks like.

Third Person POV Example

Jack traveled through a gloomy forest. Already sweat soaked his shirt. Ahead, a small ray of sunshine somehow evaded the thick umbrella of oak limbs and hone on a pile of moldy leaves. Jack ducked under a vine hanging from a tree limb and sidestepped a thick spider web.

Here we see the forest narrated by a character who uses actions and feelings to help the description: soaked shirt, ducking, sidestepping. This type of narrator brings the reader closer to the action than in the omnisicient example.

First Person POV Example

I had a sense of foreboding about the gloomy forest. Even the small shaft of sunlight ahead didn't do anything to lighten my mood. Sweat ran down my nose and dripped on my already soaked shirt. I had to duck under a drooping vine to move ahead and edge around a thick spider web.

This time, the description is even more personal and the reader is brought even closer to the forest. That is the consequence of using a first person narrator.

Omniscient POV

Writing the story using the omniscient point of view is like playing god. You, the author, know everything, see everything and even know the future of the characters. You know what each character is thinking, what his mood is and what he plans to do. To provide a graphical illustration on the omniscient POV refer to the diagram below.

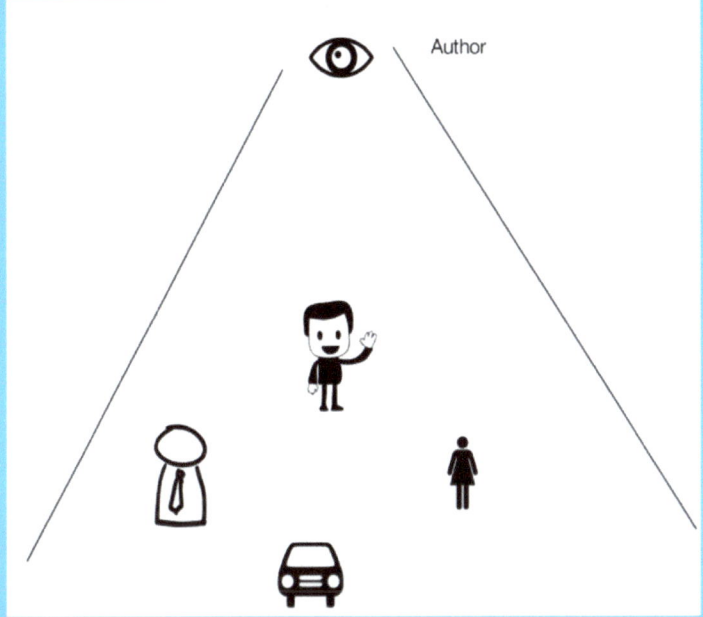

You, the author, are the eye at the top. Your all-seeing eyeball knows what each character is doing, where the car is going, who is driving it and how much mileage the car gets and you even know what is causing the strange noise in the transmission. You can jump between characters to tell the reader what each character is thinking or what the character is about to do. You can even end a scene or a chapter with the dreaded, "*Little did they know . . .*"

Third Person POV

In this point of view scheme, the narrator is a character rather than the author. The scenes are related through the eyes and ears of a character. This POV character does NOT know what the other characters are thinking or what they are about to do. The POV character can guess the others emotional state by observing their speech and body language, but this POV character does not know what is going on in their minds. That is main difference between this viewpoint and the omniscient viewpoint.

Since the reader will be spending much time with the POV characters, the readers will get emotionally involved with these characters and that is a good thing. Readers want this involvement. They want to root for the good guys and hope for the worst for the bad guys. This emotional involvement is something that is difficult to do with omniscient POV because of the distance between the story and the reader.

This sketch depicts the limited third person point of view. Character X can see what the others are doing but has no way of knowing what they are thinking.

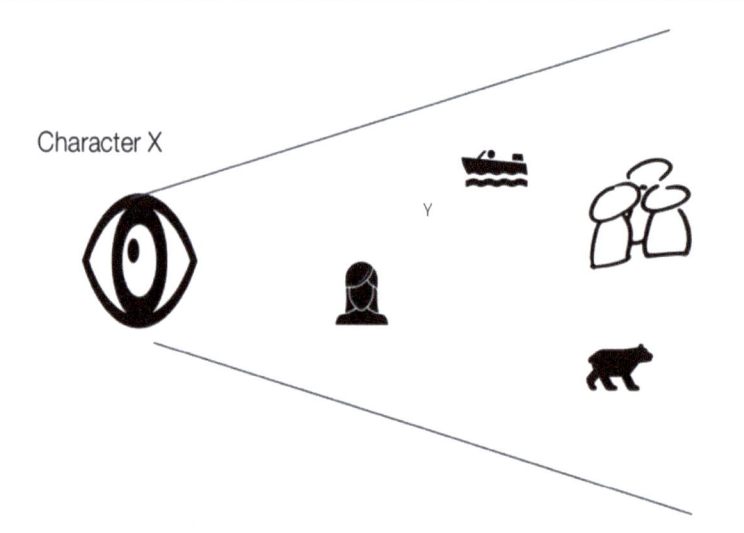

Character X

Y

The secret to writing in this POV is for the author to get inside the POV character's mind and write the scene from there. Believe me, this is strange the first few times you try it, but after a while, it becomes quite natural.

First Person POV

In first person POV, the narrator and the POV character are one and the same. The entire story is told from inside the mind of this POV character. The reader can see, hear and learn only what that POV character can see, hear and learn. For this reason the author has to get deep inside the head of this character and has to become quite intimate with the character. This type of POV is popular with mystery writers and is used in most memoirs.

Unlike third person POV, the author can't switch from a character in Manhattan to a character in San Francisco to explain what's going on out West. The Manhattan character (and the readers) won't know about the events out West unless another character tells him about the event over the phone or the Manhattan character sees it on TV. This limitation implies that the main character has to be present at all major plot events. Having a major plot event take place someplace else won't work. In this instance, the character and the reader learn about it secondhand, which is much too distant to hold the reader's interest. To use first person, the plot has to be designed in such a way that the main character is involved at each event as the plot unfolds.

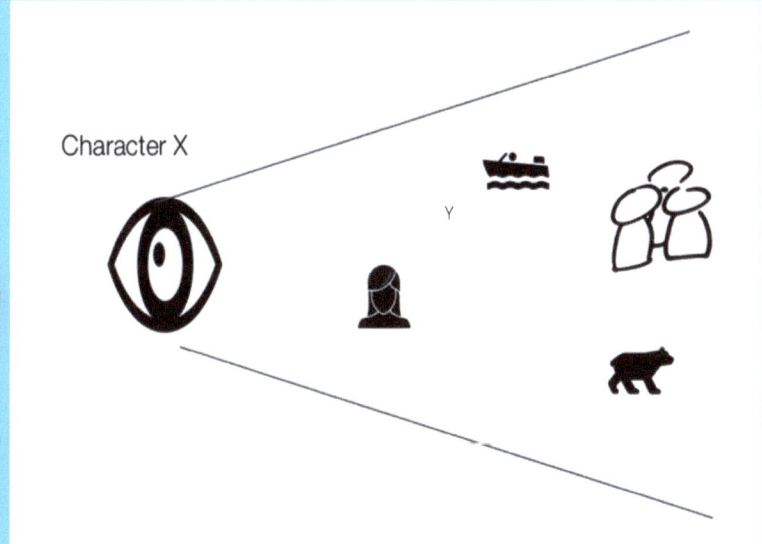

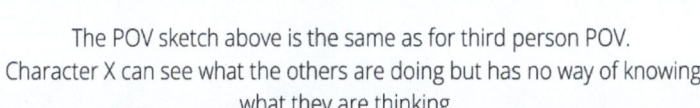
The POV sketch above is the same as for third person POV.
Character X can see what the others are doing but has no way of knowing what they are thinking.

More POV

The POV character doesn't have to be the main character. She can be the sidekick who then reports on what the main character is doing. The Sherlock Holmes books are written this way.

First person narratives are extremely personal. The author is telling the story entirely from a single POV and that means uncovering all the character's emotions, his feelings, his dislikes and his biases. At every step, the reader learns the character's motivations and attitudes. The reader must learn why the character acts and reacts the way he does. This requirement makes first person narratives more difficult to write than third person narratives.

Changing point-of-view characters is often necessary in third person POV. However there is a right way and a wrong way to do the switch.

The best way to change POV characters is to start a new scene for the new point-of-view character. Another acceptable way is to start a new paragraph within the same scene. In this case, you have to make sure the new POV character is mentioned in the first line of the new paragraph. If this method of switching is done wrong, the reader will end up with a vast amount of confusion.

The wrong way to switch POV characters is to switch in succeeding sentences. Thus, one sentence uses Jack as the POV character and in the next sentence, Bridget takes over. Then back to Jack. This scenario indicates an inexperienced writer who hasn't mastered the concept of point of view yet.

Stimulus & Reaction

Stimulus and reaction is the basic couplet of action in a story. It's a simple principle and easy to understand, yet the couplet is often done incorrectly and this leads to confusion for the reader.

It's simple ➊

The correct sequence for the couplet is 1) a stimulus occurs and 2) a reaction follows.

➋ But often done wrong

Despite the simplicity of this formula, the components are often reversed or even worse, one of the components is omitted.

The stimulus ❸

What is a stimulus? It can be a punch, a kiss, a dirty look or a pistol shot to give a few examples. It's a "happening."

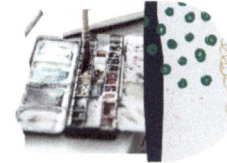

The reaction ➍

What is a reaction? It can be a defensive move, a sense of surprise, returning a dirty look or diving behind a barrel.

Next ❺

Let's examine this basic concept in more detail using examples.

Stimulus & Reaction

I'll bet you've read stories in which a character does something and you stop reading because you know you missed something. Rereading a few paragraphs doesn't fill in the blank space. The problem is the author omitted the stimulus and left you trying to figure out why the reaction occurred.

Typical Errors __ **1**

A popular version of this broken couplet is, *"Character A smiled/grinned/growled etc."* In these cases, the author doesn't bother telling us why Character A did what he did

2 __ Example-1

Jody panicked.
This is a reaction minus a stimulus

Example-2 __ **3**

Jody panicked. A dead body lay on the floor. This is better, but the reaction precedes the stimulus. Readers will probably accept this sequence because the two components are so closely related.

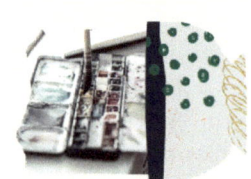

4 __ Example-3

A dead body lay on the floor. Jody panicked.
This is the correct sequence for the couplet.

Simple, eh? __ **5**

It's so simple, it's easy to do it incorrectly and not notice it. But the readers will.

Stimulus & Reaction

Let's look at some more examples of incorrect usage.

Example 1

John dived behind a barrel. A shot rang out.
Here the reaction occurs before the stimulus.

Example 2

Sally threw a drink in Alex's face.
This is a reaction, but no stimulus is shown, unless the stimulus occurred in preceding scenes and this is a delayed reaction.

Example 3

A bike ran over her foot.
Definitely a stimulus but without a reaction. This one needs an "Ouch!" or something a bit stronger

Example 4

My shoulder exploded in pain.
This one's a reaction. It'll really get the reader's attention if a stimulus isn't provided.

Got it?  5

Using the correct sequence in the couplet is a basic storytelling technique you have to master.

SHOW-DON'T-TELL

THERE ARE MANY OPPORTUNITIES FOR "SHOWING" IN ANY STORY. THE WRITER SIMPLY HAS TO UNDERSTAND HOW TO USE THEM AND HOW TO SPOT OPPORTUNITIES.

IN TELLING

the author "tells" the reader what is happening in the story or what the characters are doing.

IN SHOWING

the author lets the characters act out what is going on in the story and has the reader figure it out.

EXAMPLE 1

Telling: Jane nervously looked at her watch.
Showing: Jane shredded a paper napkin, fidgeted on her chair and glanced at her watch.

EXAMPLE 1

By telling, the author directly tells the reader what Jane's emotional state is. By showing, the author doesn't tell the reader what Jane's emotional state is. Instead the author depicts a woman acting nervously.

EXAMPLE 1

It's up to the reader to decipher the words to determine Jane's emotional state. And readers love to do this.

SHOW-DON'T-
~~~ TELL ~~~

PART OF THE JOB OF BEING AN AUTHOR IS TO
IDENTIFY SHOWING OPPORTUNITIES AND USING
THEM.

EXAMPLE 1

In this example, I've illustrated the power of showing.
It engages the reader and gets her involved in the
story. The reader is now saying to herself, "Oh, dear,
Jane is nervous about something. I wonder what is
bothering her?" In the first telling example the reader
doesn't have to do this because the author told her
about Jane's state.

EXAMPLE 2

Telling: Margo reacted angrily.
Showing: Margo scowled, placed her hands on her
hips and stamped her foot.

EXAMPLE 2

Here, the reader has to interpret the author's
words to understand what is happening.   In
this example, we see that showing always
takes more words than telling.

EXAMPLE 3

Telling: He entered the room hesitantly.
Showing: He walked through the door,
paused and looked around as if not sure
where he should go.

EXAMPLE 3

The use of an adverb often is an indication
of telling that can be converted to showing.

SHOW-DON'T-TELL

USING SHOWING WILL MAKE FOR MUCH MORE
POWERFUL WRITING AND MUCH MORE READER
ENJOYMENT. IT WILL TAKE PRACTICE TO GET
COMFORTABLE WITH SPOTTING AND REPLACING
INSTANCES OF TELLING. HOWEVER IT WILL BE WORTH
THE EFFORT.

YOUR TURN!

Convert these teling actions into
showing. This practice will hone your
writing skills. Copy the telling examples
onto a piece of paper and rewrite them
as showing.

PRACTICE 1

1. *Mary sadly watched the ambulance pull
away.*

PRACTICE 2

Chris greedily ate the hamburger

PRACTICE 3

Harry wasn't sure he should open the
package.

PRACTICE 4

"Blah, blah, blah," Agnes replied
angrily

Foreshadowing

WHAT IS IT?
Foreshadowing definition is - an indication of what is to come.

STORY APPLICATION
Used to plant clues that hint about what will happen later on in the story.

EXAMPLE
Your main character walks with a limp and uses a cane. At the climax of the story, the character pulls a sword out of the cane and this is the first time the reader sees the cane.

EXAMPLE (CONTINUED)
At this point, the story referee blows his whistle, throws a yellow flag and penalizes you 15 yards for violatng the foreshadowing rule.

THE RULE
If you need a weapon or a tool at the story's climax, you have to show the weapon or the tool to the reader prior to the climax. Several times.

Foreshadowing

WITH OBJECTS
Foreshadowing is often done with objects, especially stuff that is required in the story's climax.

WITH A CHARACTER'S BIO
You can also use material from the character's biography to foreshadow important events later in the story. As an example of this, suppose a character has a fear of open water such as a lake or the sea. This fear is based on an event when he was a five-year-old. Back then, the character almost drowned. At the climax of the story, the character is faced with a situation in which he has to save a person drowning in a lake. Does the character overcome his fear of water and save the person? Or does he walk away and hope no one saw him? Of course, to use this foreshadowing, the author has to show the character's fear of water early in the story and explain it.

CONTINUED
Another example is a fear of dark places such as caves or unlit basements. This fear could be based on a traumatic childhood experience. Naturally, the story's climax requires the character to master his fear and go into a cave.

Foreshadowing

Using a story-telling technique like these examples can greatly increase the reader's enjoyment, but the old adage holds true. You can't have a character's fear first show up at a tense moment near the end. The reader has to be shown the character's fear early on and the reader has to understand what caused it before it can be used effectively at the climax.

Foreshadowing can also be used to mislead the reader. In a mystery story, if you show a character acting suspicious, the reader will assume she has identified the guilty party. At the end, surprise the reader by revealing a different culprit. This device is widely used in mystery stories.

Foreshadowing techniques are something that must be worked out before you start to write the story. Once you know what the ending is, you can decide on the details like using foreshadowing.

METAPHORS & SIMILES

Metaphors and similes can enrich your story-telling.

METAPHOR

A metaphor is a figure of speech that directly compares one thing to another for rhetorical effect.

SIMILE

Unlike metaphors, similes create a comparison using like and as.

USAGE

When it comes to using these devices in writing, a good rule of thumb is to approach with caution and use them sparingly.

METAPHORS AND SIMILES

Examples

METAPHOR 1

Her eyes were twinkling stars.

METAPHOR 2

My phone is a dinosaur.

SIMILE 1

The teacher roared like a lion at the misbehaving classroom.

SIMILE 2

The instructions were as clear as mud.

https://examples.yourdictionary.com/

Chapter 7: Writing voice

This is the most important chapter in the book. If you do only one thing, make it this: develop a writing voice that is distinctly different from your speaking voice.

- Was and Were
- -ing words
- Adverbs
- Pronouns
- Empty words
- Naked nouns
- Horrible example

WRITING VOICE

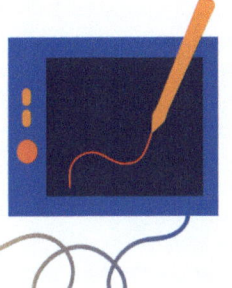

LISTEN

Try this. Eavesdrop on a conversation, one that doesn't involve you or anyone you know.

OBSERVE

What you'll observe is that the conversation is boring to anyone who doesn't know the people involved. You'll also notice that the conversation uses a lot of slang and special ways of talking.

THEREFORE

If this conversation in a speaking voice couldn't hold your interest, why would you think an entire story written in a speaking voice won't bore the readers?

BUT..

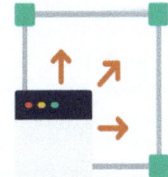

How do you develop a writing voice and what does it entail? That's what this chapter is about.

LET'S DO THIS!

"Was" and "Were"

Conversations

In any conversation, we use 'was' and 'were' in almost every sentence. While satisfactory for speaking, that makes for boring reading and bad writing.

Change

You have to develop a habit of using alternate verb constructions. Preferably, these verb constructions will use active verbs

Worth the effort

This is not easy to do, but it's well worth it. It will vastly improve your writing and that means more reader interest.

Dialog

Oddly enough, this rule doesn't apply to dialog. Why not, you may ask?

Because

dialog has to sound natural and that means using 'was' and 'were' a lot.

"WAS" AND "WERE"

Example 1
Speaking voice:
Larry was cold. He was hungry. He was also tired. He was walking along a muddy road and he was miles from home.

Example 1
Writing voice:
Larry — cold, hungry and exhausted — slogged along a muddy road miles from home.

Example 2
Speaking voice:
After I was finished in school, I was going to go home. I was going to watch that new show on TV. After that it was homework time.

The difference between the two voices is pretty dramatic, don't you think?

Example 2
Writing voice:
After school, I planned to go home, watch that new TV show and do my homework

"WAS" AND "WERE" PRACTICE

Rewrite these speaking voice
sentences using your writing voice.

01 Sally and her friends were eating breakfast.

02 John didn't know what was going on.

03 Aethelflead was Queen of Mercia and was victorious over the Viking armies.

04 Jack was sure he would go to the party.

05 The car was stuck on the side of the road.

-ing words

Another facet of our speaking voices is an addiction to -ing words. When used in writing, it gives the material an unpleasant sing-song effect.
Here is an example of what I mean:

Speaking voice

Opening the door and running down the corridor while waving her hand, she tried shouting, calling attention to her life-threatening situation.

Writing Voice

She opened the door and ran down the corridor. She shouted and waved her hand to call attention to the dangerous situation.

Exercises

Rewrite the two exercises to eliminate the -ing words.

Exercise 1

Singing really loud, I was getting hoarse.

Exercise 2

Class was boring and I was falling asleep.

ADVERBS

Adverbs are a part of our speaking voice. We tend to use them a lot.

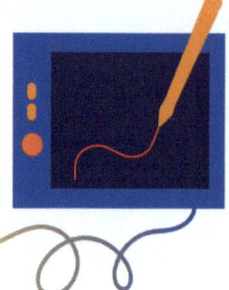

A QUOTE

The author, Stephen King, once said (or wrote) "The road to Hell is paved with adverbs."

ADVERBS

Are a useful way to write fast and produce a first draft. During the second draft, rewrite to remove the adverbs.

EXAMPLE

Sara hesitantly entered the room and slowly walked to the reception desk. She smiled wanly at the receptionist and tentatively said her name in a slightly accented voice.

REWRITTEN

Sara entered the office and spotted the reception desk. After a slight hesitation, she walked over, smiled and announced her name.

Replacing the adverbs requires some creativity and heavy thinking.

PRONOUNS

More writing voice advice

he, she, his, her, it, etc.

Another feature of the speaking voice is a limitless supply of pronouns. Often the speaker will use several pronouns in a single sentence.

Typical

Thus, it's not unusual to hear, "He said he wasn't doing it no matter what he did."

Huh?

There are three pronouns in the sentence and it's possible that each one refers to a different person.

confusion

By itself, this pronoun issue is reason enough to justify the development of a writing voice.

Change

The writing voice has to limit the pronouns and use names instead.

Empty words

In our speaking voices we use empty words, a lot of empty words. The empty words are often substituted for punctuation.

Here is a list of empty words we use in speaking: very, even, ever, really, still, just, then. And there's a lot more of them!

And there's "like" used as comma or in place of a pause.

However, sometimes these words aren't empty. On occasion they actually add meaning to a sentence. How can you tell? Use the Empty Word Test.

Empty Word Test:
Remove the word from the sentence. Did the meaning of the sentence change? If not, it's an empty word. Delete the word.

Horrible example

THE EXAMPLE BELOW IS A SPEAKING VOICE TAKEN TO THE EXTREME. IT'S NOT THAT FAR-FETCHED. I'LL BET YOU'VE HEARD PEOPLE SAY STUFF LIKE THIS.

I HAVE TO SAY, I HAD DIFFICULTY WRITING THIS EXAMPLE. MY BUILT-IN WRITING VOICE KEPT TRYING TO REWRITE IT.

JULIA WAS VERY UNHAPPY WITH HER REALLY BAD-TEMPERED AUNT AND SHOUTED AT HER JUST TO LET HER KNOW HOW REALLY MEAN SHE STILL WAS. JULIA THEN STAMPED HER BLUE-AND-WHITE SNEAKER, REALLY HARD, AND RUNNING OUT OF THE SMALL ROOM WHILE SLAMMING THE BROWN DOOR VERY LOUDLY SHE WONDERED WHY OLD PEOPLE WERE SO REALLY DUMB.

SO WHAT'S WRONG WITH ALL THESE WORDS? THEY'RE ALL PERFECTLY GOOD ONES.
I HOPE THE MATERIAL IN THIS CHAPTER HAS CONVINCED YOU OF THE NEED TO DEVELOP A WRITING VOICE THAT IS DIFFERENT FROM YOUR SPEAKING VOICE.

Chapter 8:
Putting it all
together

There is quite lot of material in the previous chapters. In this chapter, you'll see how it all fits together.

It has an eight step plan that details how to go about developing your new story.

PUTTING IT ALL TOGETHER

NOW WHAT?

So, you have all this stuff about the story you want to create. But you don't know where to start or how to use it. Don't panic. This chapter will show you how to get everything organized.

MY WAY

I've written a lot of stories and I've stumbled around looking for the best way to go about organizing the writing project.

MAYBE IT'S YOUR WAY

My way isn't the only way to go about it, but maybe it'll work for you. If it doesn't, it may give you ideas on how to develop your own way to do it.

MY APPROACH

incorporates an 8 step process that follows a logical path that will get your writing project organized .

THE PROCESS

The next page lists the steps and gives a brief description. Detailed descriptions follow.

How to create your story

using my process

Step 1

The process begins: Initial story idea, protagonist, story setting.

Step 2

Plot problem, story ending.

Step 3

Antagonist and protag & antag motivation.

Step 4

Complete the plot path, develop character arcs.

Step 5

Finish design work.

Step 6

Write first draft.

Step 7

Revise and edit.

Steps 8, 9, 10 etc.

Repeat Step 7 as many times as required.

In case you don't like lists,

here is a mind-map with
a graphical depiction
of the steps and a bit more detail.

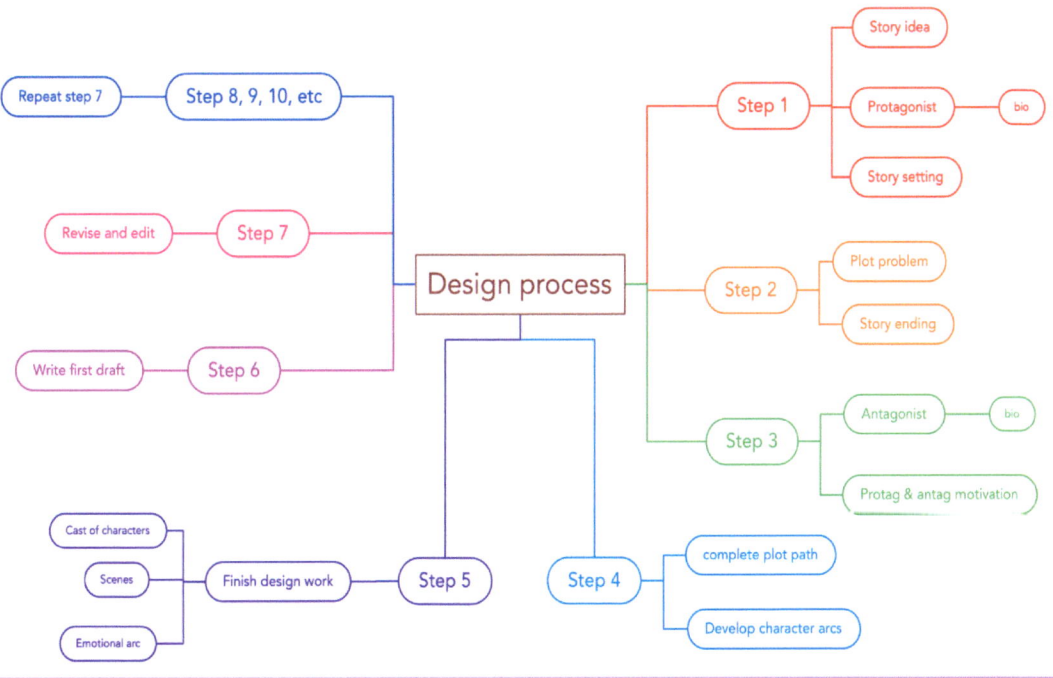

STEP 1

Starting a new story can be an exciting time.

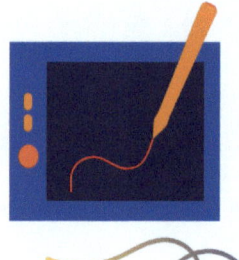

STORY IDEA

The initial story idea is what triggers the urge to create a story. Mine always starts with a character, but there are other ways to begin.

PROTAGONIST

Now you need the story's main character. Develop the character's physical and mental attributes and write a bio.

STORY SETTING

Now come up with the story setting. Mine usually involve a fantasy land or a space ship and an alien world.

THIS WILL TAKE TIME

You may not be able to develop all this material at once. Get started and as you think about what you're doing, more ideas will pop up and you can add them to the story design.

Don't get discouraged if everything doesn't fall into place immediately.

STEP 2

This step is probably the toughest one in the process.

PLOT PROBLEM

It's time to come up with the plot problem. This is what the story will be about. This is what the main characters will struggle against. In other words, it's the characters' job.

STORY ENDING

Story ideas are a dime a dozen. A story idea with an ending is worth its weight in gold. But getting the ending will take a great deal of creativity.

DO YOU BELIEVE IT?

Once you get an ending, test it. Ask yourself if you truly believe you can write a story that will go to that ending? If you don't believe in it, dump it and start over. This is an important consideration.

MAXIMUM CREATIVITY

This stuff ain't easy and it will require a lot of thinking. And maybe re-thinking.

Once you finish this step, your story will start to take shape.

STEP 3

Back to the main characters.

ANTAGONIST

To balance out the cast of characters, you need an antagonist. Who is the bad guy who will contest everything the protagonist tries to do?

CHARACTER DEVELOPMENT

Like with the protagonist, the bad guy must be completley developed with a full set of attributes and a detailed biography.

MOTIVATION

What is the motivation for the protagonist? Why does he or she feel compelled to fix the plot problem? If the plot problem involves risking his life, the motivation must be especially strong.

MORE MOTIVATION

The bad guy also needs motivation. Why does he want the protagonist to fail? This motivation must be equal in strength to the motivation for the protagonist.

If the motivations aren't equal, it won't be a fair fight.

STEP 4

More hard work requiring even more creativity.

PLOT PATH

Remember the plot cloud? Well now it's time to figure a path through that cloud. Come up with a series of events that will connect the story's beginning with the climax.

THE PATH

Must be logical and realistic. You can't conjure up a superhero to help out if you're stuck. If the characters use objects, make a note to foreshadow those objects.

PROTAGONIST ARC

With the plot worked out, now is a good time to come up with the character arc. What changed or what important lesson did she learn during the course of the story.

ANTAGONIST ARC

This character also needs an arc. Ensure it's different from the protagonist's character arc.

The arcs have to gradually develop over the course of the story. They can't just suddenly happen near the end.

STEP 5

Now for the rest of the characters and the scenes.

CAST OF CHARACTERS

Come up with more characters. Give the main characters a sidekick. Depending upon the story, you may need even more characters. Make a cast of character spreadsheet to keep track of these people. (see Chapter 3)

SCENES

With the characters and the plot in place, start thinking about the scenes you'll need to write the first draft. Remember: scenes are the building blocks of the story.

MORE SCENES

At this point, you won't come up with all the scenes you need, but you should be able to get a bunch of them. For each scene, jot down the location and what characters are in it.

STILL MORE SCENES

If you are laying out a long story, you may want to limit the scenes to only the first act of the story. Do the second and third acts later on. See Chapter 9.

This would be a good time to come up with a subplot or two.

STEP 6

Now the fun begins.

THE FIRST DRAFT

After all this hard work, it's finally time to write the story. But that hard work will make the writing much simpler than if you had to stop and figure everything out before you could proceed further.

WRITING VOICE

As much as possible, use this step as a great way to develop your writing voice. Don't write the scenes in your speaking voice! (except for the character's dialog).

WRITING SCENES

Review the material on scene design (chapter 5) to ensure the scenes you write contain the mandatory goal and emotional change. And the optional ones if appropriate.

CHAPTERS?

Your job is to write scenes and don't worry about chapters. Chapters are just a bucket to hold a bunch of scenes. You can organize the scenes and chapters later on.

If you're working on a novel, this step can take a long time. Don't expect to be done in a week or so.

STEP 7

A necessary task.

FIRST DRAFTS

Ernest Hemingway, a famous author, once wrote, "The first draft of anything is a piece of s--t." My first drafts are just that and so is yours. This may come as a shock, but you have to deal with it.

AUTO-CORRECT

Don't relay on auto-correct to catch all your typos and errors. It won't distinguish between *to*, *two* and *too*. You have to search for these mistakes.

MORE AUTO-CORRECT

Auto-correct will also mis-interpret your intentions and insert the wrong word into the story. Dig out these errors.

OTHER CHORES

While you're reading through the manuscript, look for incomplete sentences, clumsy sentence structures and other hard to read stuff.

Editing and revising isn't as excting as writing the story, but it's just as necessary. Don't skimp on the effort.

STEP 8

The end is in sight!

REVISIONS

Step 8 involves repeating Step 7. So do Steps 9, 10 etc.

POLISHING THE STORY

The first draft is just to get the story down on paper. The second draft is to clean it up. The third and fourth drafts are to shape it and polish it into something special.

READERS

After you get a third or fourth draft, it's time to ask other writers to read your story and to identify what's wrong with it. And these readers will find problems. Thank them for their efforts. Now you need still another draft, to fix all the problems.

THE FINISH LINE!

After you finish this step, your manuscript is as good as you can make it. Congratulations!

Now it's time to consider getting published. But that's another topic (and possibly another book)

Chapter 9:
Other stuff

This chapter is filled with stuff that doesn't logically fit in any of the other chapters.

- Story structure
- TAD
- Graphic stories
- World-building
- Scrivener
- Insightful issues
- Index

Story Structure

Stories have a structure.
Knowing about that structure
will simplify your job

 **The three act
structure**

Most stories

use a three act
structure although
four and even five
act stories exist.

Act 1

Is the story's opening act
and it generally contains
25% of the story.

Act 2

contains most of the
story and is 50% of
the total length.

Act 3

is the story's ending,
is 25% of the story
and includes the
climax.

Act 1

This is where the reader begins the story and this is where the author has to grab the reader's attention and convince her to read the rest of the story.

Start the main storyline and establish the story setting.

Introduce the main characters and identify a flaw in each.

Establish the starting points of the character arcs.

Add any required foreshadowing.

Begin the main subplot, if required.

Act 2

This act has the bulk of the story and contains most (if not all) of the plot events.

Continue the main story line with the plot events.

Begin the character arc development.

Add more subplots, if necessary, and continue the main subplot.

Deepen the emotional arcs.

If necessary, add more foreshadowing.

Use th

Act 3

This is the big one. The reader has stuck with the story this far and now she expects a reward. And her reward is the climax.

Wrap up all subplots.

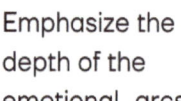

Emphasize the depth of the emotional arcs.

Write the climactic scene.

Write the validation scene and include the character arc conclusion.

Type "The end" if desired.

T.A.D.

Use this approach to write a better story.

1 ### T.A.D.

stands for Thought, Action, Dialog. Try to balance your writing so that each of the three elements are approximately equal.

2  ### Thought

This is also called internal dialog. In it, the character is thinking, usually about the situation in the story and what he'll do next.

3 ### Action

You know what this is. But the story can't exist entirely of action. There have to be breaks in the action so the reader can relax a bit.

4 ### Dialog

This is the stuff readers love. Dialog is about the characters, not the author.

5 ### Review

Keep the T.A.D. formula in mind as you write your story.

Graphic Stories

Graphic stories are popular these days and you may decide to create one. Whether you write the story or draw the story, you have to go through the story design process. Instead of writing the scenes, you draw them. Use story boards to organize your work.

Name: _____ Subject: _____ Date: _____

Title of your storyboard

A line that sets the scene....	A line that sets the scene....

A line that sets the scene....	A line that sets the scene....

For the first draft draw stick figures to get the story started, then come up with text boxes and dialog balloons. In the second draft and beyond, draw more elaborate cartoons for each scene.

There are many websites that have storyboard templates you can use.

WORLD-BUILDING

World-building is a popular activity among fantasy and sci-fi writers.

After all, their characters need a place to fight and romp around in. So, the writers create a new world, sometimes developing it in great depth. It's not unusual for the new world description to go on for thousands of words. Then, because the writer is so proud of her creation, she subjects the reader to the whole thing.

NOT GOOD! BUMMER!

The reader doesn't need to know how Mount High Point got its name. The reader doesn't need to know why it's exactly 11,239 feet high. The reader doesn't need or want to learn how Fishhook Bay came to be formed. Or why the gravity is 97% of Earth's gravity.

MOST READERS, WHEN FACED WITH A MASSIVE CHUNK OF EXPOSITION, WILL LIKELY SKIP PAST IT.

Most of the world-building consists of background information. Those details the reader needs should be spooned out in small doses, a paragraph at a time, not thousand word chunks.

SO HAVE FUN

Let your imagination go wild! Create an off-the-wall world! Load it up with crazy details. Just don't bore the reader. Pick out the important details the reader needs to know and drop those details into the story in small doses.

Scrivener

If you're serious about writing stories, you should consider getting this program or a similar one.

Manuscript
Character Re...
> Camelot
> Zaftan 31B
∨ Gundarland
  14: Law...
  15: Vigil...
  16: And...
  17: Vats...
  18: God...
  19: Bro...
∨ Negotiatio...
  20: Mes...
  21: Neg...
> old stuff
∨ Marketing
  Mktg Tem...
> Short stories
Notes
  Scene separ...
  CR title Notes
  Mktg notes
  Vella word c...
Backstory
Research
Conflicts
Trash

No Style   Verdana   Regular   12   B I U

‹ › 🚩 14: Lawsuit

The situation in Gundarland isn't good. ¶

Here is background information on it. It will help explain some of the oddities in that land. ¶

¶

❀ ❀ ❀¶

¶

Gundarland is the largest land mass on the planet called Gundar. Populated by diverse races such as dwarfs, humans, elves, half-pints, yuks and a few lesser races, these disparate races live cheek-by-jowl in many cases and get along with no more than the usual interracial hostility. ¶

At one time, the yuks roamed over all of the island subjecting everyone to their boorish behavior and crude manners. The other races mostly put up with them, but it was a brave hostess who invited a yuk to a dinner party. They ate with their fingers because they always pilfered the cutlery as soon as they sat down at the table. Eventually, the yuks were driven into the southwest corner of the island, a land of marshes and mountain deemed worthless by land developers. ¶

By ancient tradition, warriors always took a double major when they studied the arts of war. The double major came in handy during the occasional outbreaks of peace. Thus, in the middle-ages, knight-accountants, warrior-cooks and soldier-lawyers roamed the countryside seeking combat and/or clients. ¶

Details about this image are on the next page

Scrivener

In writing a story, many authors use a word processor and end up with a great many small files on their hard drive. There are character write-ups, plot notes, sketches of locations and research notes to name a few. Perhaps every scene is a separate file. Chapters may be another set of files. All of these files with their obscure file names make it difficult to retrieve information when you need it. Rearranging scenes and chapters under these conditions becomes a herculean task.

Scrivener can be used to write anything. Besides fiction and non-fiction books (it has prebuilt templates for both) it can also be used to write scripts or plays. Students can use it to write a thesis or a report.

In the graphic on the previous page, the long list on the left of the screen shows the scenes in the story grouped by chapter. The text in the middle is the scene currently being working on. Part of the problem with long stories is remembering what you said in earlier scenes or recalling whether a character has a full head of hair or is partially bald. This is especially true if the character hasn't been in a recent scene. Scrivener makes it easy to find what you need since that information is only one or two clicks away.

Another advantage with Scrivener is the ease of rearranging scenes and chapters. If you wish to move a scene from chapter ten to chapter three, all you have to do is click on the scene in the left part of the screen and drag it between chapters. Try doing that with a word processor document with all its small files.

INSIGHTFUL ISSUES

More stuff for you to deal with

1

Issue 1

How do the characters make a living? How do they play, pray, make love?

Issue 2

2

What are the politics of the world? Who has the power? At work? At home? Politics in this case isn't necessarily about national or governmental politics. Here it refers to a local level at which the story's characters operate.

Issue 3

3

What are the rituals in the world? How do the characters eat meals? How do they raise children? This issue refers to the everyday routines in the life of the characters.

Issue 4

4

What are the values in this world? What do the characters consider good? Or evil? What is right? Or wrong? What would the characters consider life is worth living for?
These questions establish the morality of the world.

In conclusion

5

Any story has questions that the author must answer in order to gain insights into the setting and the characters. This list is taken from Robert McKee's excellent book *Story*. These questions and their answers make the story more believable to the reader and hence become an important part of story-telling.

Index-2

Index-1

Write a book review?

If you found this book useful, why not tell others about it by writing a book review? Don't know how to do that? We got you covered!

How many stars, (from 1 to 5) would you give this book? (5 is the highest rating). Answer the following questions and use the answers to write a brief paragraph or two.

1) What did you like about the book?

2) What didn't you like about the book (if anything)?

3) Did the book contain information you weren't expected or didn't know about?

4) Would you recommend this book to others?

If you want, you can send your review to me and I'll post it on Amazon: hankquense (at) icloud (dot) com.

About the Author

Hank Quense writes humorous and satiric sci-fi and fantasy stories. He also writes and lectures about fiction writing and self-publishing. He has published 21 books and 50 short stories along with dozens of articles. He often lectures on fiction writing and publishing and has a series of guides covering the basics on each subject. He and his wife Pat usually vacation in another galaxy or parallel universe. They also time travel occasionally when Hank is searching for new story ideas.

Hank has a library of books, lectures, classes and other content. Visit this site to see an overview of all this stuff: https://padlet.com/hanque/6ctlburb07l0m4bv

Fiction writing is a tough business. So are self-publishing and book marketing. I have over twenty years experience in each of these fields and I've encountered all of the major pain points.
In order to help others overcome these pain points, I built the Writers & Authors Resource Center (WritersARC) website. It contains valuable content that will eliminate these pain points and provide other worthwhile information based on my personal experiences.
To see an overview of WritersARC go to
https://padlet.com/hanque/zpr8rv4gdb4iv5bn

www.ingramcontent.com/pod-product-compliance
Lightning Source LLC
Chambersburg PA
CBHW040903120626
46551CB00006B/628